D1637477

CITIES
BOSTON

ABDO
Publishing Company

Nancy Furstinger '974.4
FUR

visit us at
www.abdopub.com

CADCC

Published by ABDO Publishing Company, 4940 Viking Drive, Edina, Minnesota 55435.
Copyright © 2005 by Abdo Consulting Group, Inc. International copyrights reserved in all
countries. No part of this book may be reproduced in any form without written permission from
the publisher. The Checkerboard Library™ is a trademark and logo of ABDO Publishing
Company.

Printed in the United States.

Cover Photo: Corbis
Interior Photos: Corbis pp. 1, 5, 6-7, 11, 13, 14, 15, 16, 17, 18, 19, 21, 22, 23, 24, 25, 27, 28, 29;
    Getty Images pp. 20, 26

Series Coordinator: Jennifer R. Krueger
Editors: Jennifer R. Krueger, Megan Murphy
Art Direction & Maps: Neil Klinepier

Library of Congress Cataloging-in-Publication Data

Furstinger, Nancy.
    Boston / Nancy Furstinger.
        p. cm. -- (Cities)
    Includes index.
    ISBN 1-59197-854-8
        1. Boston (Mass.)--Juvenile literature. I. Title.

F73.33.F87 2005
974.4'61--dc22

                                                            2004052162

CONTENTS

BOSTON

Boston is the capital of Massachusetts. Although it is only 48 square miles (124 sq km), it is the largest city in New England. Boston is also the oldest city in America. It had the nation's first public library, public school, subway system, and newspaper. It was also the first city to outlaw slavery.

Boston's layout makes it a perfect city to explore on foot. Walking the Freedom Trail is a popular way to visit the many historic sites. The trail highlights places that played key roles in the **American Revolution**.

Boston blends historical and modern sites. Old churches stand next to glass skyscrapers. In the past 40 years, the city has updated many of its older neighborhoods. It has added many contemporary buildings. But, city authorities also make sure to maintain Boston's historical **architecture** as well.

The Massachusetts capital is also known for its **culture**. Greater Boston has more than 60 colleges and universities.

The Boston Symphony Orchestra, the Museum of Fine Arts, and the Boston Public Library are also found there. These institutions have earned Boston the title "Athens of America."

Quincy Market is located in Faneuil Hall Marketplace in downtown Boston. This historical area has undergone several renewal projects. The lively marketplace is known for its many shops and restaurants.

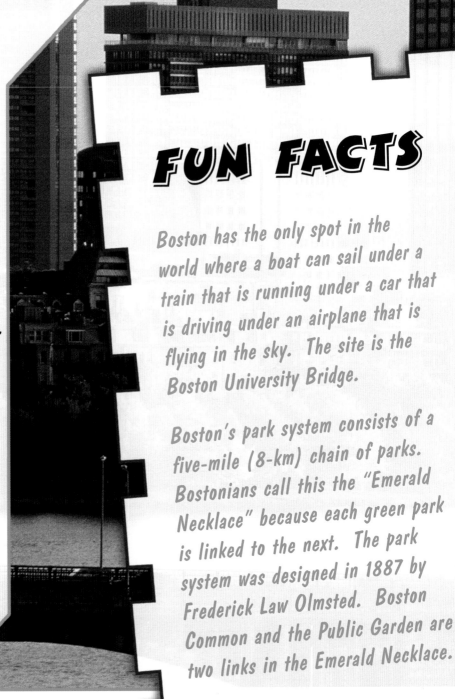

BOSTON AT A GLANCE

Date of Founding: **1630**

Population: **589,141**

Metro Area: **48 square miles (124 sq km)**

Average Temperatures:

- **49° Fahrenheit (9°C) spring**
- **71° Fahrenheit (22°C) summer**
- **55° Fahrenheit (13°C) fall**
- **31° Fahrenheit (-1°C) winter**

Annual Rainfall: **42 inches (107 cm)**

Elevation: **10 feet (3 m)**

Landmarks: **The Freedom Trail, Harvard University, Prudential Center, Boston Common**

Money: **U.S. Dollar**

Language: **English**

FUN FACTS

Boston has the only spot in the world where a boat can sail under a train that is running under a car that is driving under an airplane that is flying in the sky. The site is the Boston University Bridge.

Boston's park system consists of a five-mile (8-km) chain of parks. Bostonians call this the "Emerald Necklace" because each green park is linked to the next. The park system was designed in 1887 by Frederick Law Olmsted. Boston Common and the Public Garden are two links in the Emerald Necklace.

TIMELINE

1630 - Puritans land on the Shawmut Peninsula. They name the area Boston.

1632 - Boston is named the capital of the Massachusetts Bay Colony.

1775 - Paul Revere makes his famous midnight ride through Boston to warn the colonists that the British are coming; the American Revolution begins.

1840s - Irish immigrants begin to arrive in Boston. They are leaving Ireland to escape their country's potato famine.

1897 - The Boston subway opens.

1958 - The Freedom Trail opens.

1993 - The first Italian mayor is elected.

U.S. BIRTHPLACE

In 1630, **Puritans** sailed from England to escape religious conflict. Their first stop was Salem, Massachusetts. This town was 20 miles (32 km) north of what is now Boston. Unfortunately, water in Salem was scarce. The Puritans needed to find another place to settle.

They traveled south. At that time, Native Americans lived in the Boston area. They called the land *Shawmut*. When the Puritans arrived on the *Shawmut* **Peninsula**, the Reverend William Blackstone was the only white settler living there. He offered to share his water supply with them.

The Puritans established a settlement on the peninsula. They named their new home Boston. This was also the name of the English town where many of the Puritans had lived. In 1632, Boston became the capital of the Massachusetts Bay Colony. John Winthrop was the colony's first governor.

The colony's population increased rapidly over the next decade. There was little conflict with the Native Americans in the area. Colonists fished, built ships, and traded goods. Boston grew into a trading center for the American colonies.

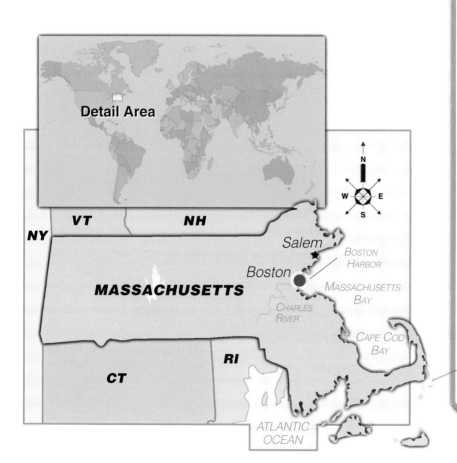

CITY ON A HILL

Boston was founded on a marshy peninsula in 1630. Three hills rose from Boston's center. The Puritans originally called their new home Trimountain because of these landforms. At this time, Boston was only connected to the mainland by a narrow strip of land. The Charles River separated the peninsula from the mainland. Boston was basically an island.

During the 1800s, Bostonians leveled two of the hills and much of what is now Beacon Hill. They used dirt from the hills to fill in the coves along the coast. Land was added to both sides of the peninsula. They also developed the mudflats and salt marshes south of the river and harbor. Bostonians created much of their city from landfill.

However, the colonists were still under the rule of the British government. In the mid-1700s, the colonists became angry when Britain taxed their goods. Taxes were placed on sugar and stamps. The colonists felt this was unfair. After all, they were not represented in England's **Parliament**.

The colonists began protesting the taxes. The king of England sent British troops to Boston to keep order. A fight broke out in 1770. Soldiers shot five colonists in the Boston Massacre.

Trouble continued in 1773 when Parliament passed the tea tax. The colonists gathered at Old South Meeting House to decide what to do. Then, Bostonians disguised as Indians boarded British ships stocked with tea. The colonists threw the tea into the harbor.

This incident became known as the Boston Tea Party. It was one of the events that prompted the **American Revolution**. In 1775, a famous revolutionary named Paul Revere rode on horseback through Boston. He warned American forces that British troops were about to attack.

The British fired the first shot of the **American Revolution** in Concord, Massachusetts, the next morning. This was called "The Shot Heard Round the World." **Minutemen** shot back at British troops. The American Revolution had begun.

American forces fought bravely against British troops. By March 1776, the patriots had forced the British out of Boston. In July, the Declaration of Independence was signed. But, it wasn't until 1783 that American independence was officially won. That year, the American colonists signed a peace treaty with Great Britain. The United States of America was born.

In this 1770 engraving of the Boston Massacre by Paul Revere, the Old State House can be seen in the background. Today, the site of the Boston Massacre is marked with a ring of stones.

FREEDOM TRAIL

Many tourists visit Boston for its rich history. They can go back in time to the **American Revolution**. The two-and-a-half-mile (4-km) Freedom Trail opened in 1958. It links the city's historic landmarks.

The Old State House is the oldest building in Boston. It is also one of the most important public buildings in America. The Declaration of Independence was read from its balcony on July 4, 1776. Just outside the Old State House, the Boston Massacre took place.

At Old South Meeting House, colonists protested the tea tax and planned the Boston Tea Party. Here, many speeches and debates determined the course of history.

Paul Revere's house is the oldest private residence in Boston. Nearby is Old North Church. There, two lanterns were hung in the steeple on the eve of the American Revolution. This was a signal to Revere to alert the colonists that the British were arriving by sea.

The Bunker Hill Monument marks the site of the battle of Bunker Hill. This was one of the earliest battles of the American Revolution.

FREEDOM TRAIL

There are 16 sites on the Freedom Trail.

1. Boston Common
2. Massachusetts State House
3. Park Street Church
4. Granary Burying Ground
5. King's Chapel
6. First public school site
7. Globe Corner Bookstore
8. Old South Meeting House
9. Old State House
10. Boston Massacre site
11. Faneuil Hall
12. Paul Revere House
13. Old North Church
14. Copp's Hill Burying Ground
15. Bunker Hill Monument
16. USS Constitution

GOVERNMENT

Boston's citizens are governed by a mayor and 13 city council members. The mayor is elected every four years. A **preliminary** election in September narrows the field of candidates to two. These two then run in the final election in November.

Boston mayor Thomas M. Menino

The council members serve two-year terms. Nine are elected to represent districts within Boston. Four represent the entire city. The city council is responsible for approving the people the mayor appoints to government positions. The council also manages the city budget.

Irish politicians have governed Boston for much of its history. When Mayor Thomas M. Menino was elected in

The Old State House in downtown Boston was the center of colonial and state government until 1798. It is now a museum.

1993, he ended a 79-year Irish winning streak. This Italian mayor began his third term in 2001. One of his goals is to give each child in Boston the best education possible.

Boston is sometimes called America's Walking City. Walking is the cheapest and easiest way to get around. Most of Boston's neighborhoods are small and friendly. So, people feel safe walking where they need to go.

Also, Boston is not an easy city to navigate by car. The downtown streets were laid out during colonial times. They are narrow and winding. Buses and automobiles crowd the narrow roads. Like many large cities, there are a lot of traffic jams.

A jetliner flies over Boston's Prudential Center (right) and John Hancock Tower after taking off from Logan International Airport.

Many Bostonians use the city's excellent public transportation system. Its subway was the first in the country. It opened in 1897. The city has a trolley system, too. Between these two modes of transportation, residents can travel anywhere in the city. There is also a **ferry** service from Boston Harbor.

Boston is the travel center of the northeastern United States. Many roads and railways fan out from the city through other New England states. Logan International is a busy airport for international and domestic flights.

South Station is a busy center for Boston's rail and subway traffic. Many people commute from nearby suburbs or smaller cities.

HIGH-TECH TOWN

In the early years, Bostonians made their living from the sea. Fishing and shipbuilding were the major industries. Today, Boston is still a center for trade. But, the city's **economy** is now based primarily on technology.

Boston's high-tech industry has been growing for 60 years. Companies produce computers, electronics, and scientific instruments such as microscopes. These firms have benefited from the latest research from local hospitals and universities.

The campus of Massachusetts Institute of Technology (MIT) is in Cambridge, a suburb of Boston. Research at MIT contributes to Boston's high-tech industry.

Today, ferries and tour boats have taken the place of fishing vessels in Boston Harbor's busy wharves.

Other major industries include food processing, clothing manufacturing, and publishing. More people are employed in printing and publishing than any other manufacturing industry. Many large banking and insurance companies have their headquarters in Boston as well.

Tourism is also one of Boston's main sources of income. The city's historical and **cultural** features attract many visitors. Its location on the waterfront also makes it a great place for boating, whale watching, or fishing.

COASTAL CLIMATE

Some years Boston winters are unseasonably warm, much like this one in January 2002.

The Charles River separates Boston from the mainland on the north and west. The river flows into Boston Harbor, which is an inlet of Massachusetts Bay. The bay empties into the Atlantic Ocean.

Because of its coastal location, Boston's weather is fairly mild. But, it can change from day to day. In fact, the entire New England region is known for its varied weather. Typically, Boston summers are hot and humid. Winters are cold and snowy. Temperatures in winter are usually just above freezing.

Spring and fall have the nicest weather, but both seasons are short. Fall is dry and cool, with November becoming cold and damp. Spring is warm and sunny, with alternating days of rain. However, it has been known to be roasting in November and freezing in June.

Weather Indicator
Visitors and natives alike can check the forecast by looking at the beacon on the John Hancock Tower (center) in Copley Square. The column of lights at the top of the building blink out a code.

- *Steady blue, clear view*
- *Steady red, rain ahead*

- *Flashing blue, clouds due*
- *Flashing red, snow instead*

During baseball season, flashing red means the Red Sox canceled their game.

BOSTONIANS

Irish clam diggers on a wharf in Boston in 1882

Boston is a melting pot of **heritages**. In the past two centuries, thousands of **immigrants** have moved to Boston. Irish and Italian are the common ancestries of many Bostonians.

A large tide of Irish immigrants arrived in the 1840s. They fled Ireland's potato **famine**. By 1920, the Irish population had increased until it made up almost one-third of the people. Italians arrived soon after the Irish. Many of them moved into the North End and East Boston neighborhoods.

Other immigrants arrived from Canada, Russia, Poland, Greece, and Scandinavia. In the early 1900s, Boston was the second most popular U.S. port of entry for new arrivals. More than 100,000 immigrants came ashore here each year during this time.

John F. Kennedy, America's thirty-fifth president, was born in the Boston suburb of Brookline. He is a descendant of Irish immigrants. Here, he stands with his Irish relatives in the Kennedys' ancestral home in Ireland.

The Irish and Italian **immigrants** were credited for bringing Roman Catholicism to Boston. The **Congregationalist** and **Unitarian-Universalist** traditions are also common religions. Many Russian Jews made their homes in Boston as well.

The redbrick town house is a famous type of Boston home. Brick houses on the cobblestone streets on Beacon Hill look frozen in time. Converted warehouses or high-rise apartments are also common residences. Many houses are rented to students.

These students attend some of Boston's highly esteemed schools. Boston University, Boston College, and

Massachusetts Institute of Technology are within the city. Harvard University, founded in 1638, is considered one of America's most respected educational institutions.

Some people visit Boston just to view its architecture. The city has preserved many historical buildings. Some of them date back to before the American Revolution. Harvard University has some of the oldest buildings in the country.

Boston is also famous for its food. Visitors shouldn't leave Boston without trying something from its seafood menu. Diners order chowders, cod, haddock, bluefish, and lobster. Boston cream pie is a favorite dessert. It is actually a cake filled with custard.

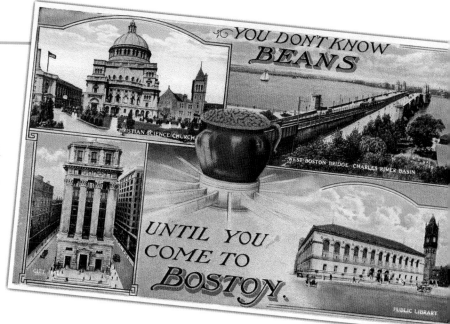

Boston's Nicknames

Boston has more nicknames than any other American city.

Cradle of Liberty - *This name represents Boston's role in the American Revolution and in helping the country gain independence from the British.*

Hub of the Universe - *Oliver Wendell Holmes, a New England author and philosopher, described the Massachusetts State House as the "hub of the solar system." People eventually used a similar phrase, "hub of the universe," to describe Boston.*

Athens of America - *Athens, Greece, was considered a center for culture and art. Because of Boston's many fine arts museums, colleges, and libraries, many people compare Boston to ancient Athens.*

Beantown - *During colonial times, Bostonians made molasses from sugar traded from the West Indies. They used the molasses to make Boston baked beans. This became one of the most popular dishes in the city. So, Boston became known as Beantown.*

Fenway Park during Game 2 of the 2004 World Series, with the Green Monster on the left. Before 2004, the Boston Red Sox hadn't won a World Series in 86 years.

Boston is a great city for sports. It has three major sports teams and two arenas where fans can watch their favorite athletes play.

The Red Sox play baseball at Fenway Park. This ballpark is the oldest and smallest in the major leagues. Fenway is home to the famous Green Monster. This is the high, green wall in left field. To this day, it continues to deny players of home runs.

Basketball and hockey fans gather at the Fleet Center. Both Boston teams have successful histories. The Celtics have won more championships than any other basketball team. The Bruins have made it to the Stanley Cup play-offs more than 17 times.

The Boston Marathon

Running and boating are also popular activities in Boston. Runners fill the streets for the 26-mile (42-km) Boston Marathon each fall. Another race, the Head of the Charles Regatta, is held on the river with about 5,000 rowers. College athletes from all over the world row 3.1 miles (5 km).

SO MUCH TO DO!

Many people visit Boston to experience its **culture**. They can watch the Boston Pops in concert on the Charles River. The Museum of Fine Arts offers exhibits of paintings, prints, and decorative art. The Boston Public Library and Harvard's libraries are considered some of the best in the world.

Boston also has several famous outdoor spaces. The Public Garden has many monuments and statues. Its most prominent statue is of George Washington. Nearby is Boston Common. It is the oldest public space in the nation. It marks the beginning of Boston's five-mile (8-km) park system.

Boston's Public Garden

Boston offers several places to see animals in their native habitat. The Franklin Park Zoo has the largest African tropical forest in the United States. Visitors learn about marine life at the New England Aquarium. It has a four-story ocean tank that holds sharks, sea turtles, and a variety of fish.

The city of Boston holds the history of the United States. Whether you visit a museum, a sports arena, or a historic spot, there is always something to do in Boston!

A 20-foot (6-m) model of a Tyrannosaurus rex can be found at the Museum of Science. Here, children can enjoy hands-on exhibits, planetarium shows, and an Omni theater.

GLOSSARY

American Revolution - from 1775 to 1783. A war for independence between Britain and its North American colonies. The colonists won and created the United States of America.

architecture - the art of planning and designing buildings. A person who designs architecture is called an architect.

Congregationalist - of or relating to a type of Protestant religion that believes the members of the church have the final authority.

culture - the customs, arts, and tools of a nation or people at a certain time.

economy - the way a nation uses its money, goods, and natural resources.

famine - a severe scarcity of food.

ferry - a boat used to carry people, goods, and vehicles across a body of water.

heritage - the handing down of something from one generation to the next.

immigrate - to enter into another country to live. A person who immigrates is called an immigrant.

minutemen - a group of armed men who were prepared to fight at a minute's notice during the American Revolution.

Parliament - England's highest lawmaking body.

peninsula - land that sticks out into water and is connected to a larger landmass.

preliminary - something that comes before.

Puritan - a person who wanted to stay in the Church of England but thought it needed some change.

Unitarian-Universalist - of or relating to a liberal, open religion with historical roots in Christianity and Judaism.

SAYING IT

Bruins - BROO-uhns
Celtics - SEHL-tihks
massacre - MA-sih-kuhr
regatta - rih-GAH-tuh
Scandinavia - skan-duh-NAY-vee-uh

WEB SITES

To learn more about Boston, visit ABDO Publishing Company on the World Wide Web at **www.abdopub.com**. Web sites about Boston are featured on our Book Links page. These links are routinely monitored and updated to provide the most current information available.

INDEX

Mindful Drinking